I0813894
Gareth Stevens
PUBLISHING
Wildly Weird
Weather
Struck by
LIGHTNING!
By Caitie McAneney

Please visit our website, www.garethstevens.com. For a free color catalog of all our high-quality books, call toll free 1-800-542-2595 or fax 1-877-542-2596.

Cataloging-in-Publication Data

Names: McAneney, Caitie.
Title: Struck by lightning! / Caitie McAneney.
Description: New York : Gareth Stevens Publishing, 2024. | Series: Wildly weird weather | Includes glossary and index.
Identifiers: ISBN 9781538288009 (pbk.) | ISBN 9781538288016 (library bound) | ISBN 9781538288023 (ebook)
Subjects: LCSH: Lightning–Juvenile literature.
Classification: LCC QC966.5 M35 2024 | DDC 551.56'32–dc23

First Edition

Published in 2024 by
Gareth Stevens Publishing
2544 Clinton St.
Buffalo, NY 14224

Designer: Corinne Eberwine
Editor: Theresa Emminizer

Photo credits: Cover Sergey Nivens/Shutterstock.com; p. 5 Vasin Lee/Shutterstock.com; p. 6 Urban Images/Shutterstock.com; p. 8 Fer Gregory/Shutterstock.com; p. 9 Menno van der Haven/Shutterstock.com; p. 10 Irina Kozorog/Shutterstock.com; p. 12 (inset) Wirestock Creators/Shutterstock.com; p. 13 Amy Johansson/Shutterstock.com; p. 14 Virrage Images/Shutterstock.com; p. 16 (inset) Mihai Simonia/Shutterstock.com; p. 17 Zaleman/Shutterstock.com; p. 19 muratart/Shutterstock.com; p. 21 Beekeepx/Shutterstock.com.

Printed in the United States of America

CPSIA compliance information: Batch #CS24GS: For further information contact Gareth Stevens, New York, New York at 1-800-542-2595.

CONTENTS

FREAKY WEATHER! 4
SPECTACULAR SPARKS 7
GONE IN A FLASH! 8
THUNDER TIME 10
HIGH HEAT 12
DEADLY BOLTS 15
LIGHTNING STRIKES 16
LIGHTNING ON THE WATER 18
STAY SAFE! 20
GLOSSARY 22
FOR MORE INFORMATION 23
INDEX 24

Words in the glossary appear in **bold** type the first time they are used in the text.

FREAKY WEATHER!

What do snowstorms, **hurricanes**, forest fires, and **volcanic eruptions** have in common? All of these weather events can cause a lot of **destruction**. Also, all of these weather events may include lightning!

Lightning is a big electrical spark. It's a great discharge, or letting go, of built-up electrical **energy**. Lightning happens in the **atmosphere** between clouds and the air, between clouds and the ground, or between and inside clouds. Lightning is common all over Earth. Sometimes it can be really wild!

THAT'S A FACT!

Each year, lightning hits the ground 25 million times just in the United States.

The longest lightning strikes in the world have measured more than 400 miles (643.7 km) across.

THAT'S A FACT!

The smallest bit of matter, an atom, is made of positive charges (protons) and negative charges (electrons).

SPECTACULAR SPARKS

How does a lightning bolt form? Ice crystals, or bits, in a storm cloud crash together. This creates a negative electrical charge at the bottom of the storm cloud. When there's enough of a negative charge built up, the energy is let go in a spark.

When it comes to charges, opposites **attract**. The negative charge in the cloud is attracted to the positive charge on the ground. Negative charge flows down to the ground and positive charge flows back up. This flow back to the cloud is the return stroke.

Lightning bolts often hit tall, pointy objects (such as towers) that are isolated, or apart, from other things.

GONE IN A FLASH!

A lightning bolt is often seen as a flash of light. The bolts come in different colors—white, blue, pink, and more. What you're seeing is the electric **current** between the ground and the cloud—the return stroke.

Benjamin Franklin helped show that lightning was electricity when he flew a kite with a key on it into a storm.

These side-to-side flashes between clouds are called spider lightning!

One kind of lighting you might see is cloud-to-ground lightning. This often looks like a zigzag between the two places. You may also see sheet lightning, in which clouds are lit up from the inside by lightning. Sometimes, lightning can travel from cloud to cloud.

THUNDER TIME

During storms, you may hear a sound that goes along with lightning. It's thunder! The light and sound of lightning are made at the same time. However, you'll see the flash before you hear the sound. That's because light travels faster than sound.

Some people and animals are afraid of thunder and lightning. That's called astraphobia.

Sometimes thunder can sound like a low rumble. Sometimes it can sound like a super-loud bang. The gap between light and sound is shorter when you're closer to the lightning strike.

Sound waves are made when the lightning's heat makes the surrounding air **expand** quickly.

HIGH HEAT

Lightning isn't only bright and loud—it's also hot! Lightning can be 50,000°F (27,760°C). That's many times hotter than the surface of the sun.

When lightning strikes some sandy beaches, it can leave behind a kind of glass called fulgurite.

fulgurite

When lightning hits a tree, it can cause the tree to explode, or blow up. It can also blow bark off the tree. This can sometimes lead to forest fires. As storms get stronger because of **climate change**, more lightning could happen, which could start more forest fires.

As some of the tallest objects in many areas, trees are perfect things for lightning to hit.

DEADLY BOLTS

Lightning sends a lot of electricity down to the ground at one time. Lightning is one of the main causes of deaths in storms. People who are hit in a direct strike may have burns and damage, or harm, to their body **systems**.

The current can jump from an object, such as a tree, to a person. That's why it's important not to take **shelter** under a tree in a storm. It can also move through the ground. That's why you shouldn't lie on the ground

If you hear thunder, get inside. Lightning can be deadly.

LIGHTNING STRIKES

Lightning can also damage property, or things people own. Trees that are struck by lightning can be cut in half or fall over. When lightning hits a building, it can travel through electrical cables, water pipes, and phone cables.

THAT'S A FACT!

As one of the tallest buildings in New York City, the Empire State Building is hit by lightning about 20 to 25 times a year.

Empire State Building

If you're on the road during a thunderstorm, stay in a car with the windows up!

People often say to get inside a car if you're outside in a thunderstorm. That's because the metal body of the car can keep you safe inside! However, if struck by lightning, the car can have damage to the tires, glass, and electrical system.

LIGHTNING ON THE WATER

Some people get caught in thunderstorms while out on the water. They might be working on a boat, swimming, or doing water sports. If you hear thunder or see lightning, it's important to get out of the water right away!

Lightning hits land more than it hits the ocean. However, when it hits water, the water acts as a conductor. That means it allows the lightning to move through it. Electricity spreads over the surface of the water. It can strike boats and people in the water.

If you're caught in the middle of the ocean in a boat or ship during a lightning storm, it's important to stay in the inside rooms, or cabins.

Park shelters are not good places to go during a thunderstorm because lightning can still strike you. 

STAY SAFE!

Remember: "When lightning roars, go indoors!" You're much safer inside than you are outside, particularly if you're on mountains or in open areas. Safe shelters include stores, cars with windows rolled up, and homes.

If you're camping or outside during a storm, leave any hills or mountains. Move away from water, such as ponds and lakes. Stay away from trees or power lines. You can **crouch** down, tuck your head in, and cover your ears. Staying smart about lightning can save a life!

THAT'S A FACT!

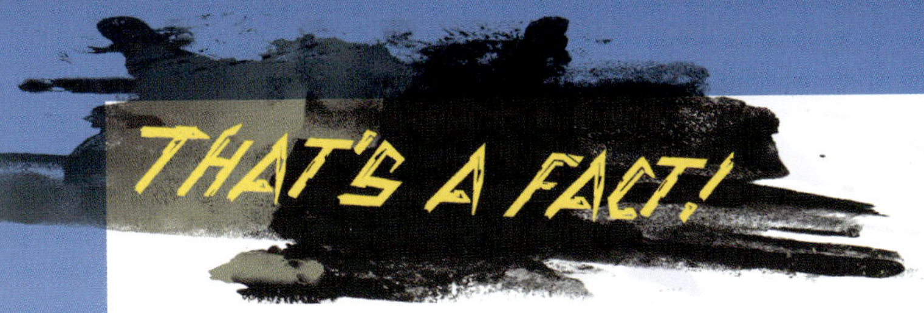

Safe shelters are buildings that are enclosed instead of open.

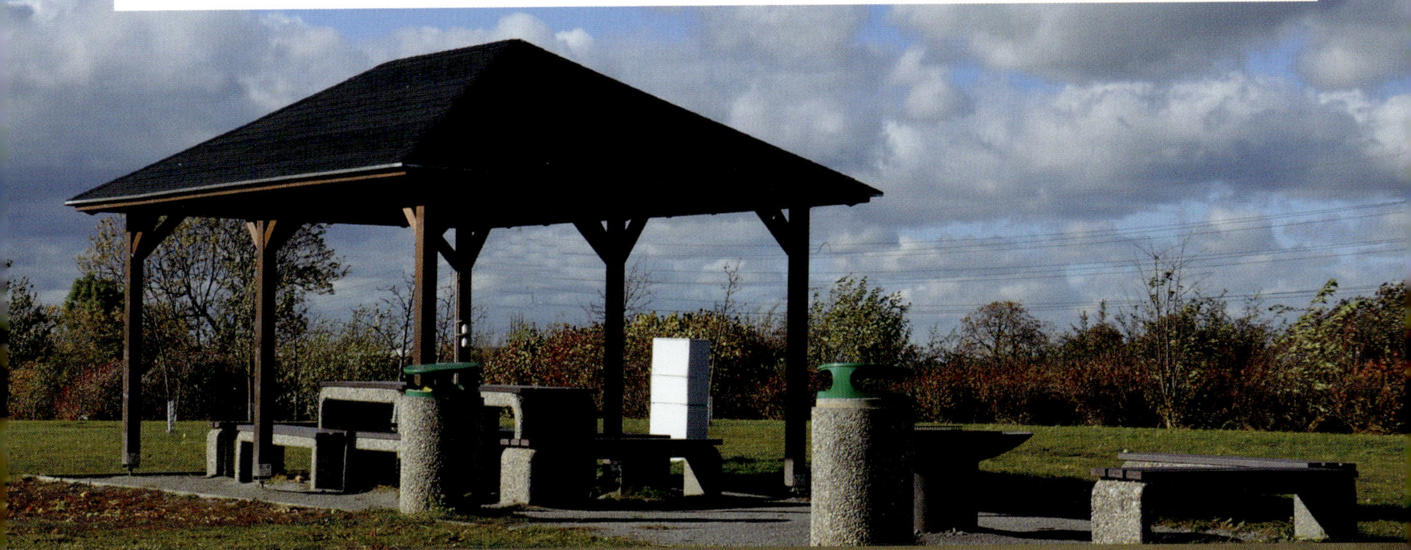

Lightning Dos and Don'ts

Do:

- Do find safe shelter indoors.
- Do stay away from open spaces, trees, and power lines.
- Do return to shore if you're out on the water.
- Do crouch low to the ground.

Don't:

- Don't take baths or showers.
- Don't use something connected to an electrical outlet.
- Don't play outside.
- Don't take cover under trees, cliffs, or park shelters.

GLOSSARY

atmosphere: The mixture of gases that surround a planet.

attract: To draw nearer.

climate change: Long-term change in Earth's climate, caused mainly by human activities such as burning oil and natural gas.

crouch: To lower the body close to the ground by bending the legs.

current: A flow of electricity resulting from the movement of particles such as electrons.

destruction: The state of being destroyed or ruined.

energy: Power used to do work.

expand: To get larger and looser.

hurricane: A powerful storm that forms over water and causes heavy rainfall and high winds.

shelter: A place where animals or people are kept safe.

system: A group of similar parts that move or work together.

volcanic eruption: The bursting forth of hot, liquid rock from within Earth.

FOR MORE INFORMATION

Books

Bender, Douglas. *Lightning*. New York, NY: Crabtree Publishing Company, 2022.

Kingston, Seth. *Lightning*. New York, NY: PowerKids Press, 2021.

Proudfit, Benjamin. *Benjamin Franklin and the Lightning Rod*. Buffalo, NY: Gareth Stevens Publishing, 2023.

Websites

Lightning
kids.nationalgeographic.com/science/article/lightning
Learn more freaky facts about lightning with National Geographic Kids!

Lightning
www.dkfindout.com/us/science/electricity/lightning/
Discover the link between lightning and electricity with DK Find Out!

When Thunder Roars, Go Indoors!
www.cdc.gov/nceh/features/lightning-safety/index.html
Explore tips for staying safe from lightning with the Centers for Disease Control and Prevention (CDC).

Publisher's note to educators and parents: Our editors have carefully reviewed these websites to ensure that they are suitable for students. Many websites change frequently, however, and we cannot guarantee that a site's future contents will continue to meet our high standards of quality and educational value. Be advised that students should be closely supervised whenever they access the internet.

INDEX

atoms, 6
cars, 17, 20
climate change, 13
clouds, 4, 7, 8, 9
color of lightning, 8
damage, 15, 16, 17
death, 15
electrical charge, 6, 7
electricity, 8, 15, 18
Empire State Building, 16
fear of lightning, 11
forest fires, 4, 13
formation of lightning, 7
Franklin, Benjamin, 8
fulgurite, 12
mountains, 20
power lines, 20, 21
return stroke, 7, 8
safety, 17, 18, 20. 21
sheet lightning, 9
shelter, 15, 20, 21
size of lightning, 5
sound waves, 10, 11
spider lightning, 9
strikes, 5, 7, 12, 15, 16, 17, 18, 20
temperature of lightning, 12
thunder, 10, 11, 15, 17, 18, 20
trees, 13, 15, 16, 20, 21
types of lightning, 9
water, 16, 18, 20, 21